STEP·BY·STEP

CHINESE
Cooking

CONFIDENT COOKING

Your Promise of Success

Welcome to the world of Confident Cooking, created for you
in our test kitchen, where recipes are double-tested by our team of
home economists to achieve a high stardard of success.

MURDOCH BOOKS®
New York • Sydney • London • Vancouver

SOUPS & STARTERS

A soup can be served during the meal or at the beginning, if preferred. A variety of little dishes or snacks are usually served as an entrée. In this chapter we give you some traditional Chinese favorites.

Spring Rolls

Ideal with drinks.

Preparation time:
35 minutes
Cooking time:
12 minutes
Makes about 24

1 package large spring roll wrappers	1/2 red bell pepper, chopped
2 dried Chinese black mushrooms, soaked	2 tablespoons cooking oil
4 ounces boneless skinless chicken breast	4 ounces bean sprouts, chopped
2 green onions, finely chopped	1 tablespoon dark soy sauce
4 ounces canned bamboo shoots, finely chopped	1/2 teaspoon sugar Oil for deep-fat frying

1 Separate wrappers. Cut each into 4 squares; cover with a cloth till needed.
2 Drain mushrooms, squeezing water from them. Remove stems and cut caps into thin strips. Set aside.
3 Finely chop chicken. In a skillet cook chicken, onions, bamboo shoots, and bell pepper in hot oil till chicken is tender and no longer pink. Add bean sprouts and cook for 30 seconds more. Stir in soy sauce and sugar; cool.
4 Place a spoonful of chicken mixture on a wrapper and fold one point over it. Fold in the two side points, then roll up towards the last point, forming a log. Moisten last point with water and press to seal.
5 Deep-fry spring rolls, a few at a time, in hot oil (375°) till golden brown. Drain on paper towels. Serve with plum sauce.

Add sugar to the cooked meat mixture with soy sauce; mix well.

Place a spoonful of the chicken mixture on a spring roll wrapper.

Fold one point over the filling and fold in the side points.

Deep-fry the spring rolls, a few at a time, till golden brown.

Prawn Toast

Serve with drinks or to start a Chinese meal.

Preparation time:
35 minutes
Cooking time:
15 minutes
Makes 36

1 green onion, white part only
2 ounces canned water chestnuts or bamboo shoots
14 ounces prawns, peeled and deveined
1 egg
2 to 3 tablespoons cold water
9 slices white bread
3/4 cup sesame seed
Oil for deep-fat frying

1 In a food processor combine onion and water chestnuts or bamboo shoots. Process till finely chopped. Add prawns, egg, and 2 tablespoons water. Process to smooth paste. Add more water, if necessary, to make spreadable.

2 Spread prawn mixture evenly over each bread slice. Remove crusts and cut each slice into 4 triangles.

3 Dip triangles into sesame seed to coat.

4 Deep-fry triangles, a few at a time, in hot oil (375°) seed side down, until light golden, turning once. Drain. Serve warm with plum sauce.

Process prawn mixture till mixture forms a smooth paste.

Spread prawn mixture evenly over each bread slice; remove crusts.

Dip triangles into sesame seed to coat.

Deep-fry a few triangles at a time till light golden.

Fried Dim Sims

*1 package wonton
  wrappers
1 pound lean ground
  pork
3 ounces canned
  bamboo shoots,
  finely chopped
1 green onion, finely
  chopped
2 tablespoons finely
  chopped fresh
  coriander or
  cilantro
2 tablespoons light
  soy sauce
Oil for deep-fat
  frying*

Preparation time:
  25 minutes
Cooking time:
  15 minutes
Makes 20 to 24

1 Cover wrappers
with a cloth till
needed.
2 In a bowl combine
pork, bamboo shoots, onion, and coriander
or cilantro. Knead
with your hands till
well combined.
3 Place a rounded
tablespoon of the
pork filling in the
center of each
wrapper. Press the
edges of the wrapper
up and around filling
to almost enclose it.
Squeeze gently so the
wrapper adheres to
the pork mixture with
the top of the pork
mixture partially
exposed and the
edges of the wrapper
almost touching on
top. Tap the base of each bundle to
flatten.
4 Fry bundles, a few
at a time, about
2 minutes or till
golden brown. Drain
on paper towels.
Serve warm with soy
sauce for dipping.

HINT
❏ If preferred, instead
of frying, steam
the dumplings for
6 minutes.
❏ This recipe also
makes about 48
wontons. Use less
filling and moisten the
edges of the wrapper.
Fold into a triangle,
pinch the edges
together, then bring
the two outer points
together. Deep-fry or
steam as above,
allowing less cooking
time than the dim sims.

*In a bowl combine pork, bamboo
shoots, onion, and coriander.*

*Knead pork mixture with your hands till
well combined.*

Place a rounded tablespoon of mixture in the center of each wonton wrapper.

Press edges of wrapper up and around filling to almost enclose it.

Crisp Quails with Pepper-Salt Dip

6 quails, halved
¼ cup dark soy sauce
2 tablespoons dry sherry
1 tablespoon finely shredded gingerroot
Oil for deep-fat frying (optional)
1 tablespoon salt
1 teaspoon Chinese peppercorns

Preparation time:
  15 minutes
Marinating time:
  4 hours
Cooking time:
  25 minutes
Serves 6 to 12

1 Rinse quails; pat dry. Arrange in single layer in a shallow baking dish. Combine soy sauce, sherry, and gingerroot. Brush over quails. Cover with plastic wrap; marinate in refrigerator 4 hours.

2 Drain quails; pat dry. Bake, uncovered, in a 400° oven for 25 minutes or till meat is tender and juices run clear. Or, deep-fry quail, a few at a time, in hot oil (375°) 5 minutes or till golden brown and juices run clear.

3 Meanwhile, heat salt in dry wok for 3 minutes over high heat. Grind salt and peppercorns till finely crushed. Pour into small serving dish.

4 Arrange quails over lettuce; serve with salt and pepper mixture.

Brush quails with a combination of soy sauce, sherry, and gingerroot.

Drain marinated quails and pat dry with paper towels.

Bake quails, uncovered, about 25 minutes or till no longer pink.

Using a mortar and pestle, grind salt and peppercorns till finely crushed.

Sweet Corn and Crabmeat Soup

Preparation time:
20 minutes
Cooking time:
10 minutes
Serves 4 to 6

2 cups frozen or canned drained corn
3¹/2 cups water
3¹/2 ounces flaked crabmeat
1 green onion, finely chopped

3 tablespoons cornstarch
2 teaspoons instant chicken bouillon granules
2 tablespoons light soy sauce

1 If using frozen corn, thaw. Place corn in a food processor; cover and process till partially ground.

2 In a saucepan combine corn, water, crabmeat, and onion. Stir in cornstarch and bouillon granules. Cook and stir till thickened. Cook and stir 2 minutes more. Stir in soy sauce.

3 To serve, pour soup into bowls and garnish with sliced green onion (green part only).

Hint
This soup is equally delicious if it is made from chopped cooked chicken instead of crabmeat.

Use a food processor to partially grind corn.

In a saucepan combine corn, water, crabmeat, and onion.

Stir in cornstarch and bouillon granules.

After soup is thickened, stir in soy sauce before serving.

Melon and Shredded Ham Soup

Preparation time:
  10 minutes
Cooking time:
  8 minutes
Serves 6

1¼ pounds Chinese winter melon or cucumbers
5 cups water
2 teaspoons instant chicken bouillon granules
4 ounces ham, cut into very thin strips
3 green onions, cut into very thin strips
2 tablespoons light soy sauce
1 tablespoon finely shredded gingerroot

1 Peel melon or cucumber and cut into thin slices, then into pieces about 1½ inches square.

2 In a large saucepan bring water and bouillon granules to a boil; add melon, ham strips, green onions, soy sauce, and gingerroot. Reduce heat. Simmer, uncovered, for 3 minutes. Serve hot.

HINT
Steamed slices of Chinese winter melon can be served as a vegetable. Toss with a little cooked crabmeat and chicken broth.

Peel winter melon and cut into thin slices, then cut into squares.

Slice ham into very thin strips.

Add ham to saucepan.

Stir in green onions, soy sauce,
and gingerroot.

Spicy Szechuan Soup

Preparation time:
35 minutes
Cooking time:
15 minutes
Serves 6

A spicy soup that's hearty and nourishing.

6 ounces firm tofu
4 ounces lean boneless pork or chicken, very thinly sliced
2 ounces lean pork or calves liver, very thinly sliced
4 dried Chinese black mushrooms, soaked
2 stalks celery, thinly sliced
1 small carrot, finely shredded
1 or 2 fresh red chilies, seeded and cut into thin strips
1 green onion, chopped
2 cloves garlic, chopped

1 tablespoon finely shredded gingerroot
2 tablespoons cooking oil
2 ounces bamboo shoots
5 cups water
2 tablespoons dark soy sauce
2 teaspoons instant chicken bouillon granules
2 tablespoons chopped fresh coriander or cilantro
1 tablespoon Chinese black vinegar
1/2 teaspoon cracked pepper
3 eggs, lightly beaten

1 Cut tofu, pork or chicken, and liver into thin slices and then into thin strips.
2 Drain mushrooms. Remove stems and cut caps into thin strips. In a saucepan cook mushrooms, celery, carrot, chilies, green onion, garlic, and gingerroot in hot oil for 2 minutes. Add bamboo shoots and pork or chicken and cook for 1 minute.
3 Add water, soy sauce, and bouillon granules. Bring to a boil; reduce heat. Simmer, uncovered, for 4 minutes.
4 Add tofu, liver, coriander or cilantro, vinegar, and pepper. Cook and stir for 2 to 3 minutes or till liver is no longer pink.
5 Slowly pour in beaten eggs, stirring till eggs form thin strands in the soup. Serve hot.

HINT

The Szechuan style of cooking is renowned for its use of fiery flavorings, mostly red chilies. This soup should have a sharp, tart taste—in fact the five flavors of traditional Szechuan foods—sweet, sour, salty, pungent, and bitter—all appear in this soup. If you prefer a less sharp taste, you can reduce the chili and pepper.

Cut tofu, pork, and liver into thin slices and then into thin strips.

Add water, soy sauce, and bouillon granules to saucepan. Bring to a boil.

Add tofu, liver, coriander, vinegar, and pepper to soup.

Slowly pour in beaten eggs, stirring till eggs form thin strands in the soup.

15

SEAFOOD

Seafood is a specialty of the eastern coastal region of China. The short, sharp stir-fry method of cooking suits shellfish and firm-fleshed fish. Green onions and gingerroot flavor seafood dishes.

Stir-Fried Prawns with Leeks

Preparation time:
12 minutes
Cooking time:
4 to 5 minutes
Serves 6

1³/₄ pounds prawns or large shrimp
2 small leeks
1 fresh red chili
1¹/₄-inch piece gingerroot
3 tablespoons cooking oil
1 tablespoon Japanese mirin or ginger wine

2 teaspoons light soy sauce
¹/₃ cup water
1 teaspoon cornstarch
¹/₂ teaspoon instant chicken bouillon granules

---

1 Peel prawns , leaving last section of the shell and the tail intact. Slit open along center of back and remove vein.

2 Cut white part of leeks into 1¹/₂-inch pieces and then lengthwise into thin strips. Remove seeds from chili and cut into thin strips. Cut gingerroot into thin strips.

3 Heat a wok or large skillet over high heat. Add oil. Stir-fry leeks, chili, and gingerroot for 40 seconds. Push to one side of wok; add prawns or shrimp and stir-fry for 2 minutes or till just done.

4 Add mirin or wine and soy sauce. Stir together water, cornstarch, and bouillon granules. Add to wok or skillet. Cook and stir till thickened and bubbly. Cook and stir 2 minutes more.

Cut white part of leeks into thin strips.
Cut gingerroot and chili into thin strips.

Push leek mixture to one side of wok;
add prawns and stir-fry for 2 minutes.

*Add mirin and soy sauce to prawn
mixture and mix well.*

*Add cornstarch mixture to prawn
mixture and cook and stir till thickened.*

Prawns in Satay Sauce

Preparation time:
20 minutes
Cooking time:
3 minutes
Serves 4

12 prawns or large shrimp
1 medium onion
2 tablespoons cooking oil
¼ cup bottled satay sauce

1 Peel prawns or shrimp, leaving the last section of shell and tails intact. Cut down center of back to remove vein. Flatten prawns or shrimp slightly.

2 Cut onion into curved slices by cutting from the top to the bottom. Separate pieces.

3 Heat a wok or large skillet over high heat. Add oil. Stir-fry onion in oil till it begins to soften. Add prawns or shrimp and stir-fry for 1 to 2 minutes or till done. Add sauce and stir till well combined. Serve immediately with hot cooked rice and Chinese greens.

HINT
This recipe is also very good when made with scallops. Wash the scallops well to get rid of sand. Halve any large scallops so they are all similar in size.

Cut onion into curved slices by cutting from the top to the bottom.

Add peeled and deveined prawns to stir-fried onions.

Stir-fry prawns and onions over high heat till prawns turn pink.

Add bottled satay sauce to prawn mixture and mix well.

Stuffed Scallops with Snow Peas

Preparation time:
  30 minutes
Cooking time:
  7 minutes
Serves 4

12 large sea scallops
1 green onion
8 ounces prawns or
  shrimp, shelled and
  deveined
1 tablespoon light
  soy sauce
2 teaspoons dry
  sherry or rice wine
1/2 cup cornstarch
Oil for deep-fat frying
2 tablespoons
  cooking oil
6 ounces fresh snow
  peas
1 teaspoon finely
  shredded gingerroot
2/3 cup water
1/2 teaspoon instant
  chicken bouillon
  granules

1 Rinse scallops; pat dry. Set aside.
2 Add white part of onion to food processor (chop and reserve green part). Cover and process till finely chopped. Add prawns or shrimp, half the soy sauce, and half the sherry. Process till smooth. Add 2 teaspoons of the cornstarch. Process till combined.
3 Generously spoon some of the prawn mixture on top of each scallop. Roll in remaining cornstarch.
4 Deep-fry scallops, a few at a time, in hot oil (375°) till brown. Drain. Drain off oil and wipe pan. Add 2 tablespoons fresh oil to pan and heat over high heat.
5 Add snow peas, gingerroot, and reserved chopped green part of onion to hot oil and stir-fry for 1 minute. Stir together water, bouillon granules, 2 teaspoons of the cornstarch, the remaining soy sauce, and remaining sherry. Add to snow pea mixture. Cook and stir till thickened and bubbly. Cook and stir 2 minutes more.
6 Place fried scallops on a serving plate. Pour snow pea mixture over scallops and serve.

Generously spoon some of the prawn mixture on top of each scallop.

Roll each stuffed scallop in cornstarch till well coated.

Deep-fry scallops, a few at a time, till brown. Drain.

Stir cornstarch mixture into stir-fried snow pea mixture. Cook till thickened.

Steamed Whole Fish

Preparation time:
35 minutes
Cooking time:
12 minutes
Serves 4 to 6

2-pound drawn red snapper or rockfish (whole fish minus its internal organs)
2 dried Chinese black mushrooms, soaked
1 small carrot
1 large green onion

¼ red bell pepper or fresh red chili
1¼-inch piece gingerroot
2 tablespoons light soy sauce
1 tablespoon cooking oil

---

1 Scale fish, if necessary. Rinse and pat dry. Make several deep cuts diagonally across body of fish on both sides.

2 Drain mushrooms, squeezing out water. Remove stems, cut caps into matchstick pieces. Cut carrot, green onion, bell pepper, and gingerroot into matchstick pieces.

3 Place the fish on a plate; scatter vegetables and gingerroot over. Combine soy sauce and oil. Pour over fish.

4 Set plate on rack in steamer. Cover, steam over simmering water about 12 minutes or until fish flakes easily with fork.

Make several deep cuts diagonally across body of the fish on both sides.

Cut mushroom, carrot, green onion, bell pepper and gingerroot into matchsticks.

Place fish on a plate and scatter vegetables and gingerroot over fish.

Pour soy sauce and oil mixture over fish. Steam about 12 minutes.

Crab in Black Bean Sauce

Preparation time:
40 minutes
Cooking time:
10 minutes
Serves 4

---

4 fresh crabs
1 medium onion
1/2 red bell pepper
1/2 green bell pepper
2 green onions
1/2 cup cooking oil
1 tablespoon finely
  chopped salted
  black beans

1 teaspoon finely
  chopped garlic
1 teaspoon finely
  chopped gingerroot
1 teaspoon sugar
1/3 cup water
1 tablespoon light
  soy sauce
2 teaspoons cornstarch

1 Cut crabs in half, then in half again. Crack large nippers with a mallet. Devein; remove fibrous tissue. Rinse crabs; pat dry.

2 Cut onion, peppers, and green onions into 3-inch strips. Heat wok over high heat. Add 1/2 cup oil.

3 Shallow-fry crab in hot oil for 3 minutes. Drain. Strain oil and return 2 tablespoons to wok. Quickly stir-fry black beans, garlic, and gingerroot. Add sugar, onions, peppers; stir-fry 2 minutes.

4 Add crab. Mix water, soy and cornstarch; add to skillet. Cook until thickened and bubbly.

Remove back flap and any grey fibrous tissue from crab body.

Shallow-fry crab pieces in hot oil for 3 minutes.

Add sugar, onion, bell peppers, and green onions to wok; stir-fry 2 minutes.

Add crab and cornstarch mixture to wok; cook and stir till thickened.

Fish Parcels

Preparation time:
  35 minutes
Cooking time:
  10 minutes
Serves 4

*1 pound white fish
  fillets
2 green onions
1 tablespoon cooking
  oil
2 tablespoons sliced
  almonds
1 tablespoon finely
  shredded gingerroot
14-ounce can straw
  mushrooms,
  drained
1/2 cup chicken broth
1/4 cup oyster sauce
1 teaspoon cornstarch
8 ounces fresh
  asparagus spears,
  cut diagonally into
  1 1/4-inch pieces*

1 Rinse fish and pat dry. Place each fish on a piece of foil large enough to enclose it.
2 Cut onions in half lengthwise and then into 1 1/2-inch pieces.
3 Heat wok over high heat. Add oil. Stir-fry onions, almonds, and gingerroot 30 seconds. Stir in mushrooms.
4 Mix broth, oyster sauce, and cornstarch. Add to wok. Cook and stir till thickened. Stir in asparagus; cool.
5 Spoon asparagus mixture over fish. Fold foil to make parcels; place in steamer basket. Cover; steam 10 minutes or until fish flakes easily with a fork.

Stir-fry onions, almonds, and gingerroot 30 seconds. Stir in mushrooms.

Stir together chicken broth, oyster sauce, and cornstarch. Add to wok.

Spoon asparagus mixture over fish fillets.

Enclose fish mixture in foil to make parcels; place in a steamer basket.

Sizzling Seafood on Crisp Rice Noodles

Preparation time:
40 minutes
Cooking time:
10 minutes
Serves 4 to 6

6 medium prawns or shrimp	**6 ounces snow peas, trimmed**
6 ounces cod or other white fish	**12 paper-thin slices gingerroot**
4 calamari tubes	**1¹/₂ cups water**
6 sea scallops	**¹/₄ cup tomato sauce**
5 ounces rice sticks or rice noodles	**1 tablespoon cornstarch**
Oil for deep-fat frying	**2 teaspoons sugar**
1 medium onion, sliced top to bottom	**1 teaspoon instant chicken bouillon granules**
1 stalk celery, sliced diagonally	**1 teaspoon chili sauce**

1 Peel prawns and devein. Cut cod into bite-size pieces. Slice calamari, halve the scallops. Set aside.
2 Fry rice sticks or noodles, in small bunches, in hot oil until they expand and turn white. Remove quickly to avoid browning and drain.

Spread noodles on a serving platter.
3 Pour off all but 3 tablespoons oil. Stir-fry onion, celery, snow peas, and gingerroot for 2 minutes. Remove from wok or skillet.
4 Add fish and seafood to hot oil. Stir-fry 1 to 2 minutes or till done. Return vegetables to wok. Spoon seafood-vegetable mixture over fried noodles.
5 Mix water, tomato sauce, cornstarch, sugar, bouillon granules and chili sauce; add to wok. Cook and stir till thickened and bubbly, then 2 minutes more. Pour over seafood mixture; serve immediately.

Peel and devein prawns, slice calamari, halve scallops, and cut up cod.

Fry rice sticks or noodles in hot oil till they expand and turn white.

Stir-fry onion, celery, snow peas, and gingerroot for 2 minutes.

Add cornstarch mixture to wok. Cook and stir till thickened.

Crabmeat Omelette

Preparation time:
  15 minutes
Cooking time:
  5 to 6 minutes
Serves 2 to 4

6 eggs
2 tablespoons light soy sauce
2 tablespoons water
Pinch each of sugar and white pepper
2 green onions, chopped
2 tablespoons cooking oil
5 ounces flaked crabmeat
1 to 2 tablespoons oyster sauce

1 In a bowl combine eggs, soy sauce, water, sugar, and pepper.
2 In a wok or skillet cook onions in oil till tender. Add crabmeat and cook for 1 minute more. Pour in egg mixture. Cook until set and light brown underneath. Cut into four wedges and turn. Cook till other side is set.
3 Transfer wedges to a warm serving plate. Drizzle with oyster sauce and garnish with green onions.

HINT
You can also make this omelette with stir-fried prawns, diced cooked chicken, or a combination of cooked meats and vegetables.

In a bowl combine eggs, soy sauce, water, sugar, and pepper.

Cook onions in oil till tender. Add crabmeat and cook for 1 minute more.

Pour in egg mixture. Cook until set and light brown underneath.

Cut omelette into four wedges and turn. Cook other side till set.

MEAT & CHICKEN

The ingredients for meat and chicken dishes should be assembled completely before beginning to cook. Sauces and seasonings are added to flavor and tenderize the meats, while vegetables are cut into even-sized pieces for stir-frying.

Sweet and Sour Pork

One of the most favored Chinese dishes.

Preparation time:
  20 minutes
Marinating time:
  20 minutes
Cooking time:
  12 minutes
Serves 4 to 6

1¹/₂ pounds pork spareribs
1 tablespoon light soy sauce
1 tablespoon dry sherry
¹/₂ medium cucumber
2 tablespoons Chinese sweet mixed pickles
1 cup cornstarch
Oil for deep-fat frying
¹/₄ green bell pepper, shredded

¹/₄ red bell pepper, cut into very thin strips
1 medium onion, sliced top to bottom
1 cup water
¹/₂ cup white vinegar
¹/₃ cup sugar
¹/₄ cup tomato sauce
1 tablespoon cornstarch
1 teaspoon instant chicken bouillon granules

---

1 Cut ribs crosswise into ¹/₂-inch strips so that each piece contains layers of pork and fat. Remove any small bones. Brush with soy sauce and sherry and set aside for 20 minutes.

2 Peel cucumber; cut in half. Scoop out seeds with a spoon and cut into thin slices. Finely chop pickles.

3 Coat pork pieces with the 1 cup cornstarch. Shake off any excess cornstarch.

4 Deep-fry pork in batches in hot oil (375°) 2 minutes or till golden brown. Drain on a rack; cool. Place 3 tablespoons of the oil in a wok. Reserve remaining hot oil to fry pork again.

5 In skillet with 3 tablespoons oil cook bell peppers and onion till tender. Add cucumber and chopped pickles and cook for 1 minute. Stir together water, vinegar, sugar, tomato sauce, cornstarch, and bouillon granules. Add to skillet. Cook and stir till thickened and bubbly. Cook and stir 2 minutes more.

6 Reheat oil for deep-frying. Deep-fry pork again in hot oil about 2 minutes or until golden brown and crisp.

7 Transfer to serving plate; spoon sauce over. Serve with rice.

Cut spareribs crosswise into $^1/_2$-inch strips and remove any small bones.

Peel cucumber; cut in half. Scoop out seeds with spoon; cut into thin slices.

Deep-fry pork in batches about 2 minutes or till golden brown.

Add water, vinegar, sugar, sauce, cornstarch, bouillon granules to skillet.

Spareribs in Black Bean Sauce

Preparation time:
  15 minutes
Cooking time:
  1 hour 40 minutes
Serves 6 to 8

2 pounds pork
  spareribs
2 tablespoons salted
  black beans, chopped
4 to 6 cloves garlic,
  chopped
2 tablespoons
  chopped gingerroot
1 fresh red chili,
  finely chopped
1½ cups water
¼ cup light soy sauce
1 tablespoon dark
  soy sauce
3 tablespoon brown
  sugar
2 tablespoons
  cooking oil
1 large onion,
  chopped
1 green bell pepper,
  chopped

1 Cut ribs into 2-inch pieces and place in an ovenproof dish. Sprinkle with black beans, garlic, gingerroot, and chili. Stir together water, soy sauces, and brown sugar. Pour over ribs.
2 Cover dish and bake ribs in a 350° oven 1½ hours or cover and place in a steamer 1½ hours or till tender.
3 Heat a wok or skillet over high heat. Add oil. Stir-fry onion and bell pepper in hot oil till tender. Add pork mixture, cook 5–6 minutes more. Serve with rice.

Sprinkle cut ribs with black beans, garlic, gingerroot, and chili.

Stir together water, soy sauces, and brown sugar. Pour over ribs.

Stir-fry onion and bell pepper in hot oil till tender.

Add cooked pork mixture to wok and cook for 5 to 6 minutes more.

Sliced Pork and Vegetables on Noodles

Preparation time:
30 minutes
Marinating time:
30 minutes
Cooking time:
15 minutes
Serves 4 to 6

---

10 ounces lean
  boneless pork
1 tablespoon cornstarch
1 tablespoon dark
  soy sauce
1 tablespoon sweet
  sherry
1 stalk celery
1/2 medium carrot
1 tablespoon cooking oil
6 small broccoli
  flowerets

6 small cauliflower
  flowerets
1/4 red bell pepper, cut
  into squares
1 small onion, sliced
  from top to bottom
1 cup chicken broth
2 teaspoons
  cornstarch
4 bundles egg noodles
2 tablespoons
  cooking oil

---

1 Cut pork into thin strips and place in a dish. Add 1 tablespoon cornstarch, soy sauce, and sherry. Mix well. Let stand 30 minutes.

2 Cut celery and carrot into matchstick pieces. Heat a wok or skillet over high heat. Add 1 tablespoon oil. Stir-fry vegetables in hot oil for 2 minutes. Remove and keep warm. Add meat and marinade to wok and cook till pork is brown. Stir together chicken broth and 2 teaspoons cornstarch. Add to pork mixture. Cook and stir till thickened and bubbly. Cook and stir 2 minutes more. Return vegetables to wok with pork, stirring to combine. Remove and keep warm.

3 Drop noodles in boiling water to soften. Drain. Add noodles to wok or skillet with 2 tablespoons hot oil. Stir-fry noodles till well coated with oil. Transfer to serving plates and spoon meat mixture over noodles.

Cut celery and carrot into matchsticks; cut broccoli and cauliflower into flowerets.

Stir together chicken broth and cornstarch. Add to pork mixture.

Briefly cook noodles in boiling water to soften. Drain well.

Stir-fry noodles till well coated with oil.

Sizzling Mongolian Lamb

12 ounces lean boneless lamb
1 tablespoon dark soy sauce
1 tablespoon dry sherry
1 tablespoon sesame oil
2 teaspoons cornstarch
2 teaspoons finely shredded gingerroot
1 teaspoon finely chopped garlic
1 large onion
2 tablespoons cooking oil
2 teaspoons sesame seed (optional)

Preparation time:
20 minutes
Marinating time:
2 hours
Cooking time:
5 to 6 minutes
Serves 4

1 Cut lamb into paper-thin slices and then into short strips. Place in a dish and add soy sauce, sherry, sesame oil, cornstarch, gingerroot, and garlic. Stir till well combined. Marinate in refrigerator for 2 hours.
2 Cut onion in curved slices from top to bottom.
3 Heat a wok over high heat. Add oil. Stir-fry onions for 1 minute. Remove. Add lamb and marinade and stir-fry lamb for 1 to 2 minutes or till done. Return onions to wok. Stir to combine. Sprinkle sesame seed over before serving.

Cut lamb into paper-thin slices and then into short strips.

Add soy sauce, sherry, sesame oil, cornstarch, gingerroot, and garlic to lamb.

Stir-fry onions in hot oil for 1 minute.

Stir-fry lamb mixture till done. Return onions to wok. Stir to combine.

Stir-Fried Beef and Broccoli

12 ounces boneless round steak
2 tablespoons light soy sauce
1 tablespoon cornstarch
1 tablespoon dry sherry
1 teaspoon sugar
4 ounces broccoli
3 tablespoons cooking oil
2 green onions, sliced
1/2 cup chicken or beef broth
1 tablespoon oyster sauce (optional)

Preparation time:
  15 minutes
Marinating time:
  30 minutes
Cooking time:
  3 to 4 minutes
Serves 4

1 Slice beef very thinly across the grain. Place in a dish. Add soy sauce, cornstarch, sherry, and sugar. Stir till well combined. Marinate 30 minutes.
2 Cut broccoli into small flowerets. Heat a wok over high heat. Add oil. Stir-fry broccoli 1 minute. Add onions and stir-fry for 30 seconds. Push to one side of wok or skillet and add the beef and marinade. Stir-fry 2 minutes or till meat turns brown.
3 Add chicken or beef broth and cook for 1 minute. Stir in oyster sauce, if desired. Serve with rice.

In a dish combine sliced beef, soy sauce, cornstarch, sherry, and sugar.

Stir-fry broccoli in oil for 1 minute. Add onions and stir-fry for 30 seconds.

Push broccoli mixture to one side of wok; add beef. Stir-fry till meat browns.

Add chicken or beef broth and cook for 1 minute.

Chicken and Bean Sprouts

- 12 ounces boneless skinless chicken breast
- 1 tablespoon light soy sauce
- 1 teaspoon sugar
- 1 teaspoon cornstarch
- 2 tablespoons cooking oil
- 3 green onions, cut into thin strips
- 4 ounces fresh bean sprouts
- 1 tablespoon dry sherry
- 1/2 cup chicken broth
- 1 teaspoon cornstarch

Preparation time:
  15 minutes
Marinating time:
  20 minutes
Cooking time:
  2 to 3 minutes
Serves 4

1 Cut chicken into thin strips, place in a dish. Add soy sauce, sugar, and 1 teaspoon cornstarch, stirring till well combined. Marinate in refrigerator for 20 minutes.

2 Heat a wok over high heat. Add oil. Stir-fry onions in oil for 30 seconds. Add chicken and marinade and stir-fry till chicken is tender. Stir in bean sprouts and sherry; stir-fry 30 seconds.

3 Stir together chicken broth and 1 teaspoon cornstarch. Add to wok and cook and stir till thickened and bubbly, then cook 2 minutes more.

Stir soy sauce mixture into chicken and marinate for 20 minutes.

Stir-fry onions in oil for 30 seconds.

Add bean sprouts and sherry to chicken mixture; stir-fry for 30 seconds.

Pour cornstarch mixture into wok and cook and stir till thickened.

Honey Chicken

Preparation time:
  10 minutes
Cooking time:
  10 minutes
Serves 4 to 6

*1 pound boneless
  skinless chicken
  breast
1 cup cornstarch
1/2 teaspoon baking
  soda
2 egg whites
Cold water
Cornstarch
Oil for deep-fat frying
3/4 cup honey
2 teaspoons sweet
  chili sauce
2 tablespoons
  sesame seed
Green onion curls*

1 Cut chicken into bite-size pieces.
2 In a bowl stir together 1 cup cornstarch and baking soda. Add egg whites and enough cold water to make a creamy batter.
3 Coat chicken in additional cornstarch and dip into batter. Deep-fry in batches in hot oil (375°) for 1 to 2 minutes or till golden brown on surface and cooked through (no longer pink). Drain.
4 In a small saucepan combine honey and chili sauce and cook over low heat till warm. Pour over chicken and serve immediately. Garnish with green onion curls.

Mix cornstarch, baking soda, egg whites and cold water to make a batter.

Coat chicken in additional cornstarch and dip into batter.

44

Deep-fry chicken in hot oil till golden brown on surface and cooked through.

To make green onion curls, cut into thin strips and place in ice water.

Stir-Fried Chicken with Peanuts and Chili

Preparation time:
15 minutes
Marinating time:
30 minutes
Cooking time:
8 minutes
Serves 4 to 6

---

12 ounces boneless skinless chicken breast
1 tablespoon dry sherry
1 tablespoon light soy sauce
1 teaspoon finely shredded gingerroot
1/2 cup cooking oil
1/2 cup raw peanuts, skins removed
1 fresh or dried red chili, sliced

1 medium onion, sliced top to bottom
1 small red bell pepper, cut into diamonds
1 small green bell pepper, cut into diamonds
1 cup bamboo shoots
1/2 cup chicken broth
2 teaspoons cornstarch
1 teaspoon chili sauce (optional)

1 Cut chicken into 3/4-inch cubes and place in a dish. Add sherry, soy sauce, and gingerroot. Mix well; marinate in refrigerator 30 minutes.
2 In a wok heat oil.

Stir-fry the peanuts and chili for 1 minute; remove, reserving oil. Pour off half of the oil. Stir-fry onion and bell peppers in hot oil for 1 minute. Push to side of pan or remove from pan. Stir-fry chicken and marinade in hot oil for 2 minutes or till chicken is no longer pink. Add bamboo shoots.
3 Stir together chicken broth and cornstarch. Add to chicken mixture. Cook and stir till thickened and bubbly. Cook and stir 2 minutes more. Add chili sauce, if desired. Return peanut mixture to skillet with chicken. Heat through.

Marinate chicken in a combination of sherry, soy sauce, and gingerroot.

Stir-fry the peanuts and chili in hot oil for 1 minute.

Push onion mixture to side of pan; add chicken and marinade.

Mix chicken broth and cornstarch. Add to chicken mixture, cook till thickened.

VEGETABLES

Vegetables are used in Chinese dishes to add color, texture, and fragrance. Red and green bell peppers, onion, and Chinese leafy greens like bok choy and Chinese broccoli are the most popular.

Cantonese Fried Rice

3 cups cold water
2 1/2 cups short grain rice
1/2 cup frozen peas
1/2 cup frozen corn
1/2 cup cooking oil
3 slices Canadian-style bacon, cut into 1/4 inch wide strips
1/2 small red bell pepper, chopped
2 green onions, chopped
2 eggs, lightly beaten
4 ounces small cooked and peeled shrimp
2 tablespoons light soy sauce

Preparation time:
 15 minutes
Cooking time:
 30 minutes
Serves 4 to 6

1 Place water and rice in a heavy large saucepan. Bring to a boil; reduce heat. Cover and simmer over very low heat and cook about 18 minutes or till rice has absorbed all the liquid and each grain is plump and separate.
2 In a small saucepan cook peas and corn in a little water till just tender; drain.
3 Heat a wok or skillet over high heat. Add half of the oil.

Stir-fry bacon till light brown around edges. Add bell pepper and green onions and stir-fry for 1 minute. Remove. Pour in beaten eggs and tilt pan to spread thinly. Cook till firm underneath. Break up egg with a spatula and remove from pan. Wipe out pan.
4 Heat remaining oil over high heat and add rice, tossing and cooking for 2 minutes. Add peas, corn, bacon, bell pepper, onion, and eggs. Add cooked shrimp and soy sauce. Cook and toss over high heat until heated throough.

Stir-fry bacon till light brown around edges. Add pepper and green onions.

Break up cooked egg with a spatula and remove from pan; wipe out pan.

Add cooked ingredients to the rice. Cook and toss till combined.

Add soy sauce and toss till well combined.

Stir-Fried Vegetable Assortment

Preparation time:
10 minutes
Cooking time:
5 minutes
Serves 4 to 6

1 medium onion	6 small broccoli
3 tablespoons	flowerets
cooking oil	6 small cauliflower
2 stalks celery,	flowerets
diagonally sliced	2 ounces bamboo
1 medium carrot,	shoots
sliced	3 ounces fresh bean
1 small zucchini,	sprouts
sliced	3/4 cup chicken broth
12 snow peas	1 tablespoon
12 straw mushrooms	cornstarch
12 ears baby corn	1 tablespoon light
8 fresh green beans,	soy sauce
sliced	

1 Halve onion and cut from top to bottom to make curved slices. Separate slices.
2 Heat a wok or skillet over high heat. Add oil. Stir-fry all vegetables in hot oil for 5 minutes or till crisp-tender.
3 Stir together chicken broth, cornstarch, and soy sauce. Add to vegetable mixture. Cook and stir till thickened and bubbly. Cook and stir 2 minutes more. Serve hot.

HINT
Other vegetables, such as bok choy, Chinese broccoli, and choy sum, can be used in this recipe. All are available from Chinese grocery stores, particularly in areas with a large Chinese population. For extra flavor add some shredded gingerroot and a dash of dry sherry to this dish.

Slice celery diagonally across the stalks.

Stir-fry all vegetables in hot oil for 5 minutes or till crisp-tender.

Stir together chicken broth, cornstarch, and soy sauce.

Add cornstarch mixture to vegetables and cook till thickened.

Chinese Vegetables with Mushrooms and Oyster Sauce

1 bunch bok choy
8 dried Chinese
  black mushrooms,
  soaked
2 tablespoons
  cooking oil
2 tablespoons oyster
  sauce

Preparation time:
  20 minutes
Cooking time:
  8 minutes
Serves 4

1 Thoroughly rinse bok choy and drain well. Cut off thick stalks and cut into thin strips.
2 Drain mushrooms. Remove stems. Simmer caps in lightly salted water for 5 minutes; drain. Cut caps into strips.
3 Bring a large pot of water to a boil. Add bok choy stems and cook for 1 to 2 minutes. Remove with a slotted spoon and drain. Add bok choy leaves and cook for 30 seconds. Remove and drain.
4 Heat a wok or large skillet over high heat. Add oil. Stir-fry bok choy stems and leaves and mushrooms for 1 to 2 minutes or till well coated in oil. Add oyster sauce, tossing to coat.

Cut off thick stalks of bok choy and cut into thin strips.

Simmer mushroom caps in lightly salted water till tender.

Add bok choy leaves to boiling water and cook for 30 seconds.

Stir-fry bok choy stems and leaves and mushrooms for 1 to 2 minutes.

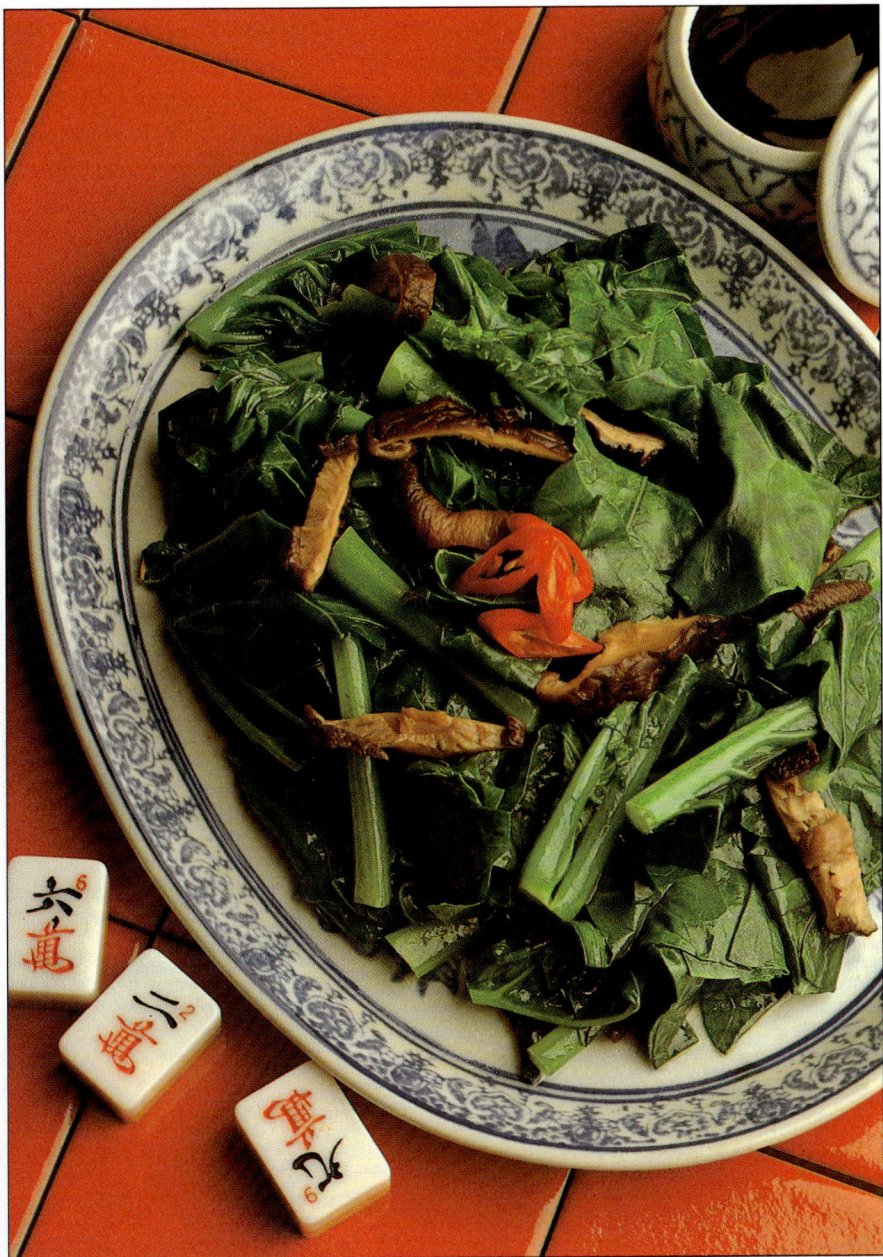

Spicy Tofu with Ground Beef

Preparation time:
20 minutes
Cooking time:
10 minutes
Serves 6

10 ounces lean ground beef
1 medium onion, chopped
2 teaspoons finely chopped garlic
2 teaspoons finely chopped gingerroot
1 tablespoon hot bean paste
1 tablespoon dark soy sauce
2 teaspoons sugar
1 pound soft tofu, cubed
3/4 cup chicken broth
1 tablespoon cornstarch
Large lettuce cups

1 In a wok cook beef and onion till meat is brown and onion is tender. Drain off fat.

Add garlic and gingerroot and cook for 1 minute. Stir in bean paste, soy sauce, and sugar and cook for 2 minutes.

2 Add tofu to meat mixture, tossing gently to combine. Stir together chicken broth and cornstarch. Add to meat mixture. Cook and stir till thickened and bubbly. Cook and stir 2 minutes more. Serve in lettuce cups; garnish with strips of red bell pepper.

In a wok cook beef and onion till meat is brown and onion is tender.

Add garlic and gingerroot to meat mixture and cook for 1 minute.

Stir in bean paste, soy sauce, and sugar and cook for 2 minutes.

Stir cornstarch mixture into meat mixture. Cook and stir till thickened.

SWEETS

Desserts as we know them are generally not served as part of a Chinese meal. Sweet treats are served as a snack or for special occasions.

Coconut Squares

2 cups water
1²/₃ cups cream of coconut
1 cup milk
¹/₂ cup sugar
1¹/₂-ounce package agar-agar powder or 1 envelope unflavored gelatin
¹/₂ cup shredded coconut

Preparation time:
15 minutes
Setting time:
1 hour
Cooking time:
5 minutes
Makes 24 squares (serves 8 to 12)

1 In a large saucepan combine water, cream of coconut, and milk. Stir in sugar and agar-agar or gelatin.
2 Bring to a boil; reduce heat. Simmer for 3 minutes, stirring constantly. Stir in coconut.
3 Pour into a wet 8- or 9-inch square baking pan. If using agar-agar, let stand at room temperature about 1 hour or till set. If using gelatin, chill about 1 hour or till set. Cut into 24 squares. Serve cold.

In a large saucepan combine water, cream of coconut, and milk.

Stir sugar and agar-agar into coconut mixture.

Stir shredded coconut into pan.

Pour into a baking pan. Let stand at room temperature 1 hour or till set.

Deep-Fried Ice Cream in Coconut

1/2 gallon vanilla ice cream
1 egg
1 cup all-purpose flour
3/4 cup water
1 1/2 cups fine dry bread crumbs
2 tablespoons shredded coconut
Oil for deep-fat frying

Preparation time:
20 minutes
Freezing time:
1 to 4 days
Cooking time:
20 seconds
Serves 6

1 Using an ice cream scoop, make 6 large scoops of ice cream. Return scoops to freezer.

2 In a bowl whisk together egg, flour, and water till smooth. In a shallow dish combine bread crumbs and coconut. Dip ice cream balls in batter and coat in bread crumb mixture. Return to freezer and freeze for 1 to 4 days.

3 Deep-fry ice cream balls, one at a time, in hot oil (375°) for a few seconds or till golden brown. Remove and drain. Serve at once.

HINT
It is crucial that the ice-cream is solidly frozen and the oil is sufficiently hot to seal and cook the bread crumb coating in just a few seconds.

Using an ice cream scoop, make 6 large scoops of ice cream.

In a bowl whisk together egg, flour, and water till smooth.

Dip ice cream in batter and coat in bread crumb mixture.

Deep-fry ice cream balls, one at a time, for a few seconds or till golden brown.

SAUCES

Here are two special sauces, ideal to serve as dipping sauces for any of the fried or steamed snacks in this book. They are both best served hot and can be covered and stored in the refrigerator for up to one week.

Sweet and Sour Sauce

1 cup water
1/2 cup white vinegar
1/2 cup sugar
3 tablespoons tomato sauce or 1/4 teaspoon red food coloring
1 tablespoon cornstarch
1 teaspoon instant chicken bouillon granules

Combine all the ingredients. Cook and stir till thickened. Cook and stir 2 minutes more.

Spicy Plum Sauce

16-ounce can whole, unpitted purple plums
1/3 cup vinegar
1 tablespoon sugar
2 teaspoons cornstarch
1/4 teaspoon five-spice powder

1 Remove pits from plums. In a food processor combine pitted plums and their liquid. Cover and process till smooth.
2 Transfer plum mixture to a

Preparation time for each recipe:
  10 minutes
Cooking time:
  5 minutes
Makes about 1/2 cup

saucepan. Stir in vinegar, sugar, cornstarch, and five-spice powder. Cook and stir till thickened and bubbly. Cook and stir 2 minutes more.

HINT
❑ For the Spicy Plum Sauce, try a little ground ginger or cinnamon.
❑ Serve both sauces with spring rolls, prawn toast, or gow gees.

For Sweet and Sour Sauce, combine water, vinegar, and sugar.

Stir in tomato sauce, cornstarch, and bouillon granules; bring to a boil.

Spicy Plum Sauce (left) and Sweet and Sour Sauce (right)

For Spicy Plum Sauce, pit plums and combine with their liquid in processor.

In a saucepan combine plums, vinegar, sugar, cornstarch, and five spice powder.

61

GLOSSARY

Agar-Agar: A type of gelatin made from seaweed. It does not require refrigeration and produces a firm jello with an interesting crunchy texture.

Bamboo Shoots: Cream-colored shoots of the bamboo plant. Sold sliced in cans. Can sometimes be bought fresh from Chinese vegetable markets. Store unused bamboo shoots in water in the refrigerator for several days.

Bean Sprouts: Creamy yellow shoots sprouted from the green mung bean (and larger, deeper yellow ones from soy beans). Soak briefly in ice water to make crisp before using. Will keep for only a few days in the refrigerator.

Black Beans: Salted and fermented soy beans which are black and soft. They are chopped to use as a salty seasoning in Chinese cooking.

Chilies/Chili Sauce: Fresh red chilies should be split open and seeded before using. Be sure to wear rubber gloves to avoid skin irritation. Hot Chinese chili sauce is sold in small bottles and should be stored in the refrigerator. Sweet chili sauce is used as a dip and in some recipes.

Chinese Green Vegetables: These vegetables look like overgrown cabbages with deep green leafy stalks. Sold at Chinese markets, they will keep in the refrigerator for several days. Cut stalks into 4-inch pieces and cook longer than leaves.

Chinese Peppercorns: Small red-brown dried berries which have a sweet fragrance and are only mildly peppery. Used whole to flavor stews and soups. Ground peppercorns are mixed with salt as a dip or condiment.

Coriander: Also known as cilantro and Chinese parsley. It is the leafy fronds of the seed spice coriander.

Corn, Baby: Tiny ears of corn sold in cans or bottles or sometimes fresh at Chinese markets. They have a pleasing crunchy texture and bland taste which makes them a popular addition to stir-fried dishes.

Five-Spice Powder: A fine spice powder made from five sweet spices – cassia, clove, fennel, star anise, and Chinese peppercorns. It is mixed with salt and used as a dip for fried foods or added as an ingredient in some recipes.

Gingerroot: The fresh root of ginger. It should be peeled and very thinly sliced or shredded. Dried ginger is not a good substitute, but crystallized ginger can be substituted for fresh.

Mushrooms, Chinese Black: These expensive dried mushrooms should be stored in a cool, dark, dry place. Soak for 20 minutes in hot water and drain before using. Trim off the hard stems and use the caps in cooking. The soaking water can be used in soups or sauces.

Noodles: Egg noodles are sold in small tangled bundles. Soak or briefly boil to untangle before using. Fresh noodles need only a brief cooking in boiling salted water.

Oyster Sauce: A thick brown salty sauce made by fermenting oysters. Always store this sauce in the refrigerator.

Rice Sticks or Noodles: Very thin whitish strands of Chinese pasta made from rice flour. Also called rice vermicelli, they should be soaked in warm water to soften and require very little cooking. To fry, do not soak and add directly to hot oil just long enough for them to expand and turn white.

Satay Sauce: This bottled sauce is made from ground roasted peanuts and spices. Store in the refrigerator.

Sesame Oil: A dark brown oil made from sesame seed which gives it a strong nutty flavor. Used in small amounts in stir-fries, marinades, and to flavor fried foods.

Sherry/Rice Wine/Ginger Wine: All of these wines are used in Chinese cooking. Dry sherry makes a good substitute.

Soy Sauce: A salty brown liquid made from fermented soy beans, wheat, water, and salt. Light soy sauce is used when a salty taste is needed and dark soy sauce is used when a dish requires a darker color.

Spring Roll Wrappers: Thin parchment-like wrappers sold in packs. Used to wrap foods before they are fried because they become very crisp. Keep damp when using by covering with a damp towel. Store unused wrappers in a freezer bag and freeze.

Straw Mushrooms: Sold in cans and sometimes fresh at Chinese markets. They are small, ball-shaped mushrooms with a mild flavor. Once opened, store them for only a few days in the refrigerator.

Tofu: Also called soybean curd, it is made from soy bean milk by a process similar to cheese making. Tofu has a custard-like texture with a bland taste. Soft tofu is added to soups, meats, and vegetable dishes. Firm tofu is sliced for frying or added to braised dishes. Once opened, store in the refrigerator covered with water, for up to one week.

Vegetable Oil: A mild oil used for deep-frying. Chinese cooks prefer to use "cooked" oil for stir-frying. This is vegetable oil that has been used once or twice for deep-frying and has lost its "raw" taste.

Vinegar, Chinese Black: Sold in Chinese markets, it is dark and mild tasting. A good substitute is malt vinegar or cider vinegar diluted with a little water.

Water Chestnuts: Small round crisp vegetables sold in cans and fresh at Chinese markets. They have a crunchy texture and a bland, slightly sweet taste. Store covered in water in a container in refrigerator for several days.

Wonton Wrappers: Small thin squares of pasta dough, made from egg and flour. Can be stored in the refrigerator for several days.

INDEX

Numbers in italics refer to pictures.